Life

Love

&

Living

My thoughts……

Poetry

By Joyce A. Nash

Contents

<u>Acknowledgements</u>

I am amazed on how God blessed me to write these poems and I acknowledge His authority in this book. These poems were written to give life, laugh and love. I pray you find something or everything that will make you smile or shed a tear of truth.

Enjoy,

Joyce

<u>Introduction</u>

Poetry is defined as "literary work in which special intensity is given to the expression of feelings and ideas by the use of distinctive style and rhythm; poems collectively or as a genre of literature."

Poetry can be an expression of life that reaches the heart to another's.

Poetry doesn't always have a rhyming tone, but have a deep meaning stimulating the mind, reaching the soul and transcending into the heart.

In this book you will find poetry that God has given me in different aspects of life, love and living.

Some familiar, some funny and some make you think, but heartfelt.

I am also introducing **Saraiyah Shearon Hughes**, a budding poet in the making.

<u>Waterfalls</u>

Waterfalls rushes into my soul,

removing debris to make me whole.

Each drop beats at my heart,

demanding change from the start.

Waterfalls, Waterfalls, you flow with design,

changing courses that keeps me in line.

Roaring, dashing, flashing and tear,

in my mind, why am I here?

Waterfalls, Waterfalls, answer me please,

I can only help you on bended knees.

Waterfalls don't end where they began,

cleansing down deep within,

Leaving me refreshed, renewed and revived

making me grateful that I am alive.

Waterfalls, waterfalls are you done?

No, washing and changing you is so much fun!

Waterfalls, waterfalls, all over me,

loosening stains for me to be free.

Waterfalls strength, power and incomparable force,

dashing, crashing, rolling while staying on course.

(2)
<u>Porches</u>

Standing, bending, looking around,

waiting sometimes to be found.

Porches, sturdy, big and small,

rails, designs and without walls.

Entrances to the left, middle and right,

watching how to make my flight.

Planning, escaping from this life,

so much turmoil, hatred and strife.

Porches usually don't hold much glory,

but years of unspoken and unwritten stories.

History of many things unseen,

some are dark and chilling to the spleen.

Porches have wisdom, words one needs to hear,

laughter, crying and a lot of fears.

Porches holds captives in their minds,

never to leave what is behind.

Memories of good of whatever is left,

sometimes haunting tales on each step.

Porches have passed through so many skies,

hearing bountiful truths and so many lies.

Porches.

(3)

<u>Love</u>

Is there a poem on such a subject?

One we have not heard?

A song that has not been sung?

That melts the heart with every word.

Lyrics written in the middle of the night,

that drives the heartbeat to a flight.

Strings, drums, tunes and vibes,

that brings the heartbeat much alive.

Love! We all want to feel!

Nothing fake, phony and totally real.

Funneling down into the depth of the soul,

breathless and melting us on the floor.

Love, like seeds needs cultivating and time,

to grow and mature like that aged old wine.

Love, a subject with no end,

with power to stop the hatred within.

Love is not just to make us glee,

but to capture man's heart to be free.

The price for love is an opened heart,

in you and in me, that is where it starts.

(4)

<u>Liquid drops</u>

Liquid drops silently rolling down the cheek,
unparalleled lines forming in every streak.
Liquid drops forms in groups on its own,
unspoken words forming its own tone.
Liquid drops, liquid drops, drip, drip, drop,
from the ducts it cannot stop.
Liquid drops, liquid drops I wish to control,
turns itself on ever so bold.
Liquid drops, liquid drops like a stream,
revealing the heart, what does that mean?
Life don't always block the heart from pain,
that is the chance we take again and again.
Liquid drops are not always the tears of life,
sometimes it is a joy from a baby or a wife.
Liquid drops, liquid drops rise from the heart,
form its own path and work its own art.
Liquid drops speak the truth with each tear,
rolling gently without any fear.
Liquid drops, liquid drops, relieves our eyes,
from the pressure the heart hides.

(5)

Lessons from the leaf

There are lessons to be learned from the leaf,

such as what to do with the heat?

It bears the warmth of the radiant sun,

because it knows the day will be done.

Heat helps the leaf to grow,

lessons that we humans know.

We love the coolness of the shade,

but the heat is how we are made.

(6)

The language of fall

Leaves changing speaks to our lives,

reminding us we too will change in time.

The grass and air change its song,

that seasons change and doesn't stay long.

(7)

I. leaf

I. Leaf, change colors indicating diversity,

not understanding the hatred of humanity.

There is beauty in difference and such glory,

learn from the leaf, it tells its own story.

Signed, **I. Leaf**

<u>**(8)**</u>

<u>Candy wrapper</u>

Chewy, gummy, can't wait to eat,

that delectable sugar we so much seek.

Chocolate, nuts, and nougat delight,

crunchy, chewy with each bite.

The joy having such an exquisite cuisine!

Our mouths watering and rolling,

you know what I mean.

The wonder of having such a great time,

what's in the wrapper is mine, all mine.

But we forget the most important piece

the candy wrapper to say the least!

The process it takes to hold it all,

yet, the candy wrapper seems so small.

Made in different shapes, sizes and colors,

the candy wrapper is like none other.

Flexible, bendable, sturdy and true,

but the treasure inside is our view.

The pleasure of the prize!

Here it comes, open wide!

Candy wrapper finally acknowledge at last,

it has a moment of glory, before it hits the trash.

<u>(9)</u>

<u>Laugh</u>

I laughed for my first child, I wanted one,

I laughed for my second, and this is fun.

I laughed at the third, believing it's a lie,

the fourth and fifth, I said goodbye.

I didn't laugh.

<u>(10)</u>

<u>Life like a pickle</u>

Life is like a pickle, so crazy and fickle:

the kosher: life is good.

the dill: sometimes it's silly.

the hot: testing and trials.

the garlic: close your mouth and smile.

the sweet & spicy: life has its twist.

the candied: being kind is sometimes a risk.

the bread and butter: do what you got to do.

Cucumbers wished we would understand,

the changes it endures getting into our hands.

The jarring, pickling it goes through,

to experience the crunchy ecstasy of the chew.

Because if you think life is sometimes a fickle,

take a look at the process of a pickle.

(11)

My son and ADHD

I twitch, I twirl, I talk, and I stand,

I am trying to sit as best as I can.

Please get to know me, so I can have a chance.

I see, I hear and sometimes comprehend,

it just takes a little time to zero in.

I need space and time to be who I am,

Please get to know me, so I can have a chance.

My days can be good and sometimes not,

but when I am at my best, I am red hot!

Numbers sometimes don't make sense,

and words clumps like bushes in a fence.

Please don't judge me by those things alone,

and yes, I work better when I am left alone.

I AM full of creativity and my mind knows it,

pull it out of me, so I can show it.

No, I am not like others and I only me.

I am a unique person, let me be free.

Thank you for listening and please understand,

All I ever wanted is to be given a chance.

And there are things could be missing,

but please take time to sit and listen.

<u>(12)</u>

<u>Pain</u>

There are not enough words for pain,

who has the strength to explain?

Words spoken don't always do justice,

for what happened and how it left us.

Heartaches singing in the middle of the night,

still feeling like darkness even in the light.

I can talk, I can say, I can cry what I feel,

for the pain to say "I am here still."

Days turn into months, months into years,

pain, why are you still here?

Every time I am willing to go,

your memory invites me back, you know.

We often want pain to leave and stay gone,

but continue in singing its hurt song.

It is not pain fault that it stays a while.

it is often cuddled like a little child.

And pain doesn't designate a time to leave,

it waits upon us through the grief.

Pain? "I'm still here."

Waiting to exit without your fear,

that I will be back.

<u>(13)</u>

<u>The Soul</u>

The soul is like a deep, deep well,

it's hard to know and who can tell?

Written like poetry with an endless pen,

stroking letters with no end.

Long sentences and winding words,

up and down, so many swerves.

Transcribing symbols, deciphering marks,

things embedded, deep in the heart.

The soul knows the years of its journey,

pain and tears sometimes deeply buried.

Powerful and creative the soul can be,

unfolding mysteries to make one believe.

Resurrecting dreams, bringing hope to life,

the soul has power to make it right.

Turning the tides of tragedy and tears,

the soul, when strong battles fears.

The laughter and joy in the end,

often brings smiles and grins,

when it knows the sorrow has an end.

The soul is vibrant and full of life,

a mystery, beautiful evolving in time.

<u>(14)</u>

<u>Oh, that filter!</u>

I try not to say and even hold my tongue,

to let the battle stay won.

But my filter……

I bit my lip and try to find,

a place in me to be kind.

But my filter……

If I walk away and turn my head,

it will be over, I hope, I said.

Walking fast towards the door,

quickly I need a few steps more.

But it came out like a fountain,

like an avalanche on a mountain.

Vowels, consonants, nouns and verbs,

unleashing thoughts, oh those words!

Things that can't go back in the mouth,

my that filter can really go south!

Oh, the regret of voicing our minds,

those words don't always heal in time.

Before I thought of the alphabets spilled,

and the room was totally filled.

With that filter……

<u>**(15)**</u>

<u>I want to be me</u>

It was never a race to live this life,

to rush to have a husband or wife.

The thrust of society made us to believe,

you have to have such things to be received.

But life was created for us to be the one,

what God intended through His Son.

Not to be clones of a popular magazine,

telling us how to look so thin and lean.

The outward appearance divides us apart,

but never disclose the truth of the heart.

That sometimes life is not cracked up to be,

I just really wanted to be me.

Not man's opinions with defining lines,

trying to make and mold me time after time.

Telling me I'm not, I can't, I won't be,

what they perceive that really isn't me.

Changing my story to fit their script,

never thinking that it won't fit.

I am me already penned to the end.

Thank you, but I like being me.

(16)

Silence

Is it true that silence is golden?

words from the heart not unfolding.

Sitting and glancing without imparting lips,

if I speak, what sound will it rip?

Silence sometimes is a good friend,

it can be a weapon, it all depends.

Silence and quietness are two different things,

one is deeper, if you know what I mean.

Quiet may say "I still want to talk",

Silence may say, "Go take a walk."

Silence can be dangerous at times,

What is really going on in the mind?

How we wish we could open and see,

what is really stirring beneath.

What are you thinking, please tell us so?

Do you really want to know?

I am not sure you want me to release,

I am silent for the sake of peace.

Cease for the words that you seek,

for the answer may be bleak.

Because silence do not speak.

<u>**(17)**</u>

<u>Bellissimo (Beautiful)</u>

Fare noi veramente conoscere "Bellissimo?"

Fare noi veramente avere un traccia?

Qualche volta bellissimo è al di là me and tu.

Why is beautiful considered the eyes, lips and hair,

when beauty can be seen everywhere.

Just look beyond what you see,

the abundance of discoveries.

Did you know roses had so many species?

About 150, if you please.

Roses with many colors have their own story,

unfolding petals in its glory.

Bellissimo!

Sunrises of orange and yellow streaking so bold,

make the heavens look like liquid gold.

Waterfalls running over hills and mountains,

Untamable, majestic, beautiful fountains.

Two hearts fusing together in love for eternity,

becoming one in unity is life mystery.

Noi ancora non conoscere,

Come in profondità esso va!

Bellissimo!

Bellissmo!

(18)

Slavery

You took my son with a gun,

I knew then I was done.

I bowed my head in untold pain,

knowing I will never see him again.

My daughter reached while being torn,

from the only place she knew, my arms.

I could not touch and comfort her soul,

she need not watch me be killed dead cold.

I had to surrender and that's all I could give,

in order for their souls to live.

And I was angry, mad and afraid,

of the thought saying "this is where I laid."

All sort of things goes through one mind,

if I can snatch them and run in time.

Maybe in the middle of the night,

I can make a daring flight.

Or by some chance they run back to me,

they found a way to be free!

Years has passed and my eyes grown dim,

my heart has stopped, I will never see them again.

Now I am six feet under………

<u>(19)</u>

<u>God's Creations</u>

The Planets, the Universe and the Stars are some of

God's creations.

God also created Adam and Eve.

God made Adam from the dirt and Eve from Adam's rib.

God made trees, rivers, forest, and food that I and you

eat today.

He made the Ocean were fish come from.

He made the Chickens and animals.

He even made you, your family and your friends.

God's creations are beautiful.

-Saraiyah Shearon Hughes

Nov 4th, 2018

<u>**(20)**</u>
When is it time to go?

When it's time to go, you will know.

Like the summer breeze, the rustling of the leaves.

Like the ice cream truck that's on time,

the season has changed, don't you hear the chimes?

Like the changing of the clothing in the stores,

in comes the new and out goes the old!

When is it time to go?

I tell you; you will know.

Like the pendant missing from a chain,

replacing it, is not the same.

When love no longer covers your soul,

once was a fire, is now so cold.

When it is time to go? you will know.

The arms that was once opened, becomes full of self,

once was welcomed, now it's less help.

When is it time to let go?

When you no longer hear the heartbeat,

and love is not tender and sweet.

When eyes don't meet, crossing one another,

and communication goes no further.

It's time.

<u>(21)</u>

<u>Writer's Block</u>

What do I write, where do I start?

Forming sentences can be hard.

What am I saying, does it make sense?

Dabbling, scribbling, until it clicks.

Should I say this or mention that?

Like pulling ten rabbits out of a hat.

I'll write about something very deep!

Only to find out it puts people to sleep.

What about my past, my history?

If there is a great interest in me.

Writer's block is hard while trying to jot and tittle

only to find out, you wrote just a little.

The sentences seem much in your mind,

only three words, what a waste of time!

Give me a word, a phrase or two,

I need to finish; I want to be through.

Does anyone else have pen issues?

I'm not crying, please pass the tissue.

Then it happens, in the wee hours of the morn,

a thought, an idea, a paragraph is born!

The flow of words because the block is gone!

(22)

Being Young Again

Being young again are days of fun,

whispering winds, welcoming the sun.

Rising early to gather friends on the way,

laughter always saving the day.

No agenda, no set time,

wandering through the day, being free in mind.

When hopscotch was math and we didn't know it,

playing freeze was our mannequin, move and blow it.

Corner stores took our nickels and pennies,

licorice, chips, eating candy was plenty.

Finding new adventures in the neighborhood,

marking secret places where we gather and stood.

Didn't understand the green stamp collection,

but we made sure we kept them in protection.

Hot days that caused for the hose,

water all over us, even up our nose.

Being young again, some people would dismiss,

tragedies, pain, they don't want to remanence.

If we had the power, to go back in time,

many things we would change, that shaped our minds.

One is youth is not being an adult before our time.

<u>(23)</u>

<u>If I could change this world</u>

If I could change this world,

I would stop babies from being torn from the uterus that

needs to be born.

If I could change this world,

I would stop the fist of that person who is hitting and has

determined not to miss.

If I could change this world,

I would make people understand that we all have a death

date, so live as God planned.

If I could change this world,

I would shelter children hearts from the stolen innocence

that has torn them apart.

If I could change this world,

I would want men to see that we all play a part in this

universe to be free.

If I can change this world, but I can plainly see,

I can't change the world, God did not leave that to me,

He sent His Son Jesus for men to have peace,

To have love for humanity and harmony.

That is how the world changes,

this how we become free.

<u>About the Author</u>

Joyce A. Nash is a minister over Hadassah Ministries founded in 1999 with a newsletter entitled *"Notable."* The mission is for women to be empowered in all five areas of life: physically, spiritually, naturally, emotionally and financially through God's word and holistic teaching.

Women seminars and teachings was birthed in 2009.

In 2017, Minister Joyce received her B.A. in Communications and became the author of **"Spiritual Carbon Monoxide"** which can be purchased on **Amazon.com** or sent to you by request at: **hadassah1999@yahoo.com**

Hadassah blogpost can be found on Hadassah2012.blogspot.com.
Teaching videos of Minister Joyce can be found on **FB: Hadassah Ministries and/or Minister Joyce A. Nash**. *"Notable"* and *"Girl, I Need a Word"* are publications of Hadassah Ministries.

She is the mother of two college graduates and both called to fulfill destiny.

Hadassah Ministries is registered with the State of Missouri. All publication is under Hadassah Ministries.

www.ingramcontent.com/pod-product-compliance
Lightning Source LLC
Chambersburg PA
CBHW051014050726
47592CB00007B/2851